AF488912

IF YOU ARE NOT

SEEN

YOU ARE

LOST

"IT TAKES 3 SECONDS TO GET NOTICED"

MEGHAVI VYAS

Copyright ©2020
bizHQ – An Imprint of Kalon Maple Publishing

author asserts the moral right to be identified as the source of this work.
All Rights Reserved by Kalon Maple Publishings BIZ HQ.
No part of this publication may be reproduced, stored in a retrieval
system or transmitted in any form or by any means, electronic,
mechanical, photocopying, recording or otherwise, without the
prior permission.

First Published in August 2020

Published By:
bizHQ
An imprint of Kalon Maple Publishing
+91 9665 609 444

ISBN: 978-81-946992-0-0
Price: 199₹

Layout Design, Cover Design:
Mrunaal Gawhande

Editor: Vivek Gawhande

Distributed by:
Paperback: amazon.com, amazon.in, flipkart,
kalonmaplepublishing.com
E-Book: amazon.in/com, apple (ibooks stores in 51 countries), barnes &
noble (us and uk), scribd, kobo, and blio, overdrive (world's largest
library ebook platform serving 20,000 + libraries), baker & taylor axis
360, tolino, gardners, Google Play Books, bibliotheca cloud library
(3,000 public libraries) and odilo (2,100 public libraries in north america,
south america and europe) + paperback

This book is dedicated to

Men and Women in

Uniform from

Indian Army

Indian Air Force

Indian Navy

On 15th August 2020

We are because You are

In Gratitude

WHY SHOULD YOU READ THIS BOOK?

Brian Tracy quoted, 'Many capable men and women are disqualified from the jobs they deserve, just because they do not look the part" And this is a little more evident when it comes to us as Indians. Unfortunate but a bitter truth to be swallowed hard. This book is a tool to, *look the part*

With many things happening across the country I had been reading a lot about people who have been contributing immensely. I often found myself asking this question, *"If I had to contribute my share what can that be?"* After a bit of thinking I could figure out that in my limited capacity I can at least bring about a change in the professional image we all carry as Indians. In spite of being power house of talent we are overlooked at times just because we fail to create an impact. This is where most of the people lose confidence and succumb to the situations. Let us not forget, *'The first step to be respected is looking respectable'*. With our system that puts more stress on values, intent and education we somewhere lack in self-presentation. Often we cover it in the name of humility.

After knowing the importance of our values, intent, education which is the core, now is the time we also work on our self-presentation. Globalization has made this the need of the hour and to be the next super power we need to work on this.

This is a book written with a thought to give out some information for image management keeping in mind the professional scenario. It has been written in a simple manner with handy tips. The entire concept of professional image has been broken in four components in an easy to remember way, A–B–C–D, which is **Appearance**, **Behavior**, **Communication** and **Digital** Presence. Further each section of A–B–C–D contains amazing yet easy to implement tips. To wrap up each of the A–B–C–D section we have three power moves of each listed towards the end. You may just randomly open up any page and you will find a take away.

Lastly, read it because I have written it for you. You can always gift it to someone if you have outgrown the tips this book has to offer. Either consume or contribute: that is how you can look at it.

WORD OF ACCLAIM

I believed myself to be a savvy dresser right upto the time I entered the corporate world. Having joined the Indian Navy right after graduating as an engineer, I spent the next seven years following the protocols. We had very specific uniform for each occasion including parties, dinners and even sports. Post my service, when I entered the corporate world, I was actually made aware of the term "Power Dressing".

In hindsight, I can only wish that, I would have had a book like this. Megha you have so simply but effectively put together, all I have learned over the years. Belonging to the fast moving corporate world, I can confirm that your suggestions are bang on. The language is simple but articulate and as a reader one can instantly connect.

I absolutely loved your statement " We Dress to Express"! It is a very empowering and empathetic statement. Your simile of accessories likened to vitamins is truly inspired and the suggestion to "Play the game" when it comes to work place rules is a must for success.

Finally, creating awareness about the digital footprint is the need of the hour. I wish you success with regards to this book not just for your sake but also for the millions of lives it can supportively impact.

A must read for all....there is surely something for everyone in this book

LtCdr Pawan Desai
– Co-founder & CEO, MitKat Advisory Services

'**If You Are Not Seen You Are Lost**' by **Meghavi Vyas** is an enticing read and a step by step guide on a subject that is much coveted; how to become a better person, professionally and socially. This book takes it a notch higher; it also aims at guiding people who guide people.

Finest of the fine details have been touched upon by the author which give you a sense of deja vu at multiple occasions. The homework done on basic human psychology which often passes under the radar is so precise that it tends you, either a professional aspirant or a mere casual reader to agree with everything the author means to express.

It is almost like you become a better and a more impressive person midway through the book.

People from all walks of life, especially the ones looking to make a name for themselves must give it a go. This compelling read might be the stitch that saves your nine.

The debutant writer is very convincing and actually writes like a seasoned wordsmith.

In her own words, don't just read this book, absorb it. If you don't, you might live to rue it.

Sergeant Lavraj Singh Kanyal.
Indian AirForce

I have known Meghavi for last four years and have seen her work. Her presentations to some huge Malaysian corporations were well received.

What this book has to offer is something I think every individual needs to understand and know.

We often underestimate the power of Image we exhibit, but dealing with global audiences for my work, I can vouch for the fact that first impression and Image is vital and this book is the easiest way to understand it.

My heartiest congratulations to Ms Meghavi Vyas on the launch of this very useful and handy guide.

Divine blessings.

Bharat K. Ajmera
Global President
- International Entrepreneur Chamber, Malaysia
VIce President - United Association of all Indian NGOs

We've heard many times – make your presence felt! It would mean different things for different people however Meghavi has beautifully brought out the DNA of 'how to make your presence felt and contribute positively towards your own impression getting formed by the other person.

If you're a postgraduate student wanting to step into the professional world or if you're already into corporate life or business or profession, this book is for you! As an executive coach, I have observed that many brilliant minds lose out on how they show up, communicate, their clothing etc. No longer can you be careless about what and how other people think of you!

As Malcom Forbes said "Presence is more than just being there"! This book expands that topic for you.

Meghavi has canned her years of experience in this painstaking effort. I enjoyed reading this book and invite you to dive into the world of authentic image building and polishing, your executive presence and much more!

Take a test! Just check how you're feeling right now before reading this book and check-in on your feelings again after reading it, you'll notice the positive difference. Just like I did.

- Ujjaval K Buch, MCC
Master Certified Coach, International Coaching
Federation, USA and Director, United Minds

'If You Are Not Seen, You Are Lost'.... how simple but how true!

This book is a fantastic reflection of Meghavi's experience of over a decade now, in the field of Personal grooming and brand building.

We are all as professionals, offering differentiated competitive products and services to our clients and customers. We therefore need to know the professional tricks to position & market our brand if we wish to win the competitive battle of emotions in the client's mind.

Simple as it may sound, it is critical. It's how you want others to think and feel about you as a boss, a coworker, a candidate, a friend or as a business partner.

Often when I have personally been confused at my personal branding levels, I have sought her reconfirmation. Her tips & advise have always been very useful. This booklet of personal brand building wisdom will help you a lot. I would say just invest your time and read it.

In a world of social networking, if you are not on Linkedin, you will be lost for want of meaningful links. The bird that does not tweet is unknown in the garden. If you are not heard, you are unknown.

And if you are not seen, you are lost!

Adil Malia

– A co- traveller, friend, a colleague, a mentor

"...approximately 93% of how people judge us when meeting face-to-face is decided upon our non-verbal presentation..." is the statement which forced me to read whole book, **If you are not SEEN You are LOST** by Ms. Meghavi Vyas.

Since I met her and now while reading her book, I can connect the way she molded herself professionally and the same knowledge; based on her experience of change, she had penned for all of us. One of the best things about the book is, I am sure once you start you will complete it in one go. It seems as if the book is talking about our own day to day life experiences. The content has been simplified to the highest form, hence allowing common man to access the knowledge of Image Management.

These 9000 words may look simple but let me share a small observation with you all. These words are highly effective and serve as eye opener to make us realise the difference we can bring in our personality.

Meghavi, along with habits, attitude, and behavior has taken a note of digital world as well. We perceive we are different professionally and personally; however we need to bridge this gap and present ourselves as a holistic individual – online and offline.

I would suggest, close your eyes, get ready with pen and paper, think for a while how you perceive yourself and others, write it down and then read and feel the immediate difference.

My all best wishes with you, Meghavi for such a noble work (Guide paper) putting your experience for others. God bless you with all success....

Dr. Haresh Chaturvedi
V.P. Human Resources. Reliance Industries, Dahej.

"Image is everything." A phrase agreed by all but confused by many!!! The biggest misconception is "Image" as a term considered only for an exterior appearance. Image is actually is an internal manifestation through external expressions. This piece exactly captures that. An interesting read if one wants to get strong from inside out. A good confidence builder!!!

Sanjay Nair
President – ImageIO

FOREWORD

"It's time to get noticed"

Image is the **representation** of the external form of a person; the 'representation' in the neural circuitry, in the brain. Visual impression is instant and long lasting in minds of people. Such memory holds for longer duration in the brain. Though, appearance alone will never determine success but it plays a major role in your success. It is not about being good-looking but 'looking-good'. Your Image is the stepping stone to success.

Meghavi Vyas a Civil engineer transformed to be an **Image Management Consultant**, due to her deep core passion for design: designing personalities, carving out the uniqueness of an individual to be one's brand onto the mission of assisting aspirants to create their image, their brand and be a potential image consultant.

Her book - : **If you are not SEEN you are LOST"**, is not just a book but her dream, her passion, driven out of her value and experience of a decade. Knowing her personally at professional level, I take pride and privilege in expressing her passion and authenticity as an Image Management Consultant.

The book is a tool loaded with strategies intended for a journey towards positive change, towards growth. It is expressed in a simple, comprehensive manner: to be a ready reckoner for image makeover. The spontaneity and comforting flow of the book will compel you to ponder over the precise and insightful 100+ tips to make the powerful first impression. The book lays out holistic and comprehensive approach of ABCD of an individual's image as Appearance (how do you look), Behavior (how you act), Communication (how you talk) and Digital Presence (Web Presence)

The book so convincingly corroborates that, **'you are noticed, the moment you are seen'** and this plays a pivotal role in our lives. The 'Image" is measured / represented in the way one is seen. Studies suggest that while meeting face to face, the body language and the way one presents oneself (the non-verbal conversations) amount to approximately 93% as to impression invariably becomes the important framework of the personality. At no point does the appearance takes over the words, however the three seconds notice, to be seen gets to steal the opportunity.

An Image Management Consultant mentors, guides and addresses fashion, and as well, goes far beyond in articulating personal and professional image for all times by empowering with confidence and competence. It may not matter as to at which stage or what state of life one is, everyone must invest with an Image Management Consultant to build confidence, grow and succeed in life.

A must possess book with every human being.

No one could have been better than Meghavi to roll out this element of "Image Management"

"You never get a second chance to create a First Impression"

Best Wishes,

Brigadier Jayant Tiwari, Shaurya Chakra (Retd.)
Life Leadership Excellence Coach,
Leadership Mentor, OD Strategist, Speaker

ACKNOWLEDGMENT

Many thanks to:

Almighty for blessing me with all the resources I needed to pen this book. Many thanks to the endless support of my parents and family, without which I would have never thought of doing what I am doing.

This moment takes me at least a decade back when I was allured by the concept of Image Management but I wasn't sure if I was a fit for it or not. In this state of confusion but deep resonance with the concept, it was my lovely friend, Sheetal Shah, and her husband Rajan Shah who supported me in my – at that time crazy – the decision of getting into this. Without their support, I would have never been an Image Management Consultant.

I would also like to acknowledge the Image Consulting Business Institute for the fantastic learning and support I got. My journey was not easy getting the technical concepts of Image Management elements in my head.

I had doubts, at times I felt I took a wrong decision; I was stressed about the time, money, and energy I invested. Once, I had a serious thought to quit this program halfway so that I can at least save half of my investment. (I am sure I will not be judged for being vulnerable) however, Almighty had different plans for me.

Once I got certified, the comfort of the classroom vanished. While I was feeling absolutely clueless and lost, I have gifted the gem of mentors, Jassiji, Mr. Jaswinder Pal Singh or Just Win Singh as popularly known. If it was Sheetal who helped me take the plunge, Jassiji was the one who helped me sail through. Moments of despair became moments of delight with his help. For this duo, my words will always fall short to express my gratitude.

2017 was the time I again fell in love with Image Management when I went for my International certification to Conselle, Utah – USA. The robust learning from none other than Ms. Judith Rasband, the grandmother of the industry made me realize the depth of the concept. I developed a deeper and holistic approach to the subject. Those days were not just spent learning the lessons of image management but they were life-changing days. Judith was one educator who taught more with conduct than she did with words. The warmth for her learners, the passion and dedication for the subject, she would at times have teary eyes when she talked about it. I wish I could imbibe a fraction of those attributes from her. And more than anything else, her willingness to educate her learners was something I recall before any session even today.

I would like to acknowledge all the educators who transformed me to be what I am today.

Mrs. Suman Agarwal – a living example of perfection, for the teachings on Image, which is the core of my domain.

Mr. Shyam Kumar – who taught how to transfer the knowledge and skills over to the learners. His unique way of teaching has its own impact.

Mr. Maanveer Singh – the person who walked his talk – for teaching us the life lessons.

Ms. Deepali Nair – the magic box, the first person to induce that confidence and hope in me that I can be on the other side, I can be an educator.

How can I forget lovely Nicola Bhardwaj and Devanshi Gandhi who gave us practical learning?

Vadodara ICBI for the support, my batch mates, my learners who helped me be on my toes and kept me abreast of the subject.

My acknowledgment remains incomplete without the mention of the man behind this entire inspirational journey, none other but the founder of Image Consulting Business Institute, Mr. Rakesh Agarwal. Not coming from a business background, not having any business degree or business sense for that matter, a huge part of my success goes to the guiding light provided by him. The simplicity and clarity with immense calmness and consistency have taught huge business and life lessons, not just to me but thousands in the fraternity. Had it not been for his wisdom, my technical knowledge would have accompanied me in my afterlife.

My career as an Image Management Consultant lies on a tripod with three strong pillars, Ms. Judith Rasband, Mr. Rakesh Agarwal, Mr. SHyam Kumar. They are my roots!! And they are so strong that I need not worry about the flowers and fruits.

These were the major pillars I would want to acknowledge, however as a civil engineer, I know it is not only the columns that sustain the structure, we need beams, walls, and other support as well.

It would be difficult to list all the friends and other support I got for writing this book, but to mention a few, Akash Garg, who helped me put this dream of writing my book in action, Neha Bhatt, who inspired me to write with simplicity since she does not like to read, Jogesh Jain, the silent motivation always there to help when needed, Mrunaal who helped me make my dream come true to publish it on independence day, in spite of short notice.

Seeking love and blessings,

In Gratitude,
Meghavi Vyas

CONTENTS

INTRODUCTION

CHAPTER 1 – APPEARANCE

CHAPTER 2 – BEHAVIOUR

CHAPTER 3 – COMMUNICATION

CHAPTER 4 - DIGITAL PRESENCE

ABOUT THE AUTHOR

INTRODUCTION

Now that I am penning down this book, the world is going through hard times. An unknown virus; now called Coronavirus has struck the world and people are suffering from a strange and unknown disease named Covid – 2019. With no other alternatives known, world is in a lockdown, but not me. I am rather cocooning and that is how this book – a long conceived dream of mine is in your hands.

Hi, my name is Meghavi Vyas and I am an individual who moved from engineering buildings to engineering personalities. Yes, you got it right!! I am a Civil engineer who is now turned to an Image Management Consultant. The yesteryears of my life, I was the one who badly needed an Image Consultant and today I am an author to the same subject. Instead of taking services, I render services; I help aspirants to gear up to be a potential image consultant. It is easy to pen down those thousands of words for my book, **"If you are not SEEN you are LOST"**, but I don't have enough words to express my gratitude for being able to do this. A big thank you to you too, **my reader** for holding my book in your hands.

It is not just a book but my dream, my passion, my sweat, my sleepless nights, my exhausted mind that you are holding. Out of my experience of a decade I can think of three distinct reasons why this book is in your hands.

ONE you are a loving family member, encouraging friend, an admirer, maybe my learner-sometimes back and this is your gesture to support me and my endeavor. I am ever so grateful to you and your encouragement. My heart is filled with love and respect for you.

TWO you are trying to figure out what is this being noticed and 130 strategies and all of this stuff and how does this relate to your success? Your curiosity has got your hands on this book and let me challenge you with all love and respect, don't keep it down half way. This book definitely has something for your curious mind. Just stick around.

THREE you want to simply check out what have I written?!! You probably know me; but randomly. You are surprised hence you want to check this out. Go ahead and do it; but lovingly.

IDEAS FOR ~~READING~~ ABSORBING THIS BOOK

They say there has never been an escalator to take you to success. Stairs is the only way. This stands true for the thoughts expressed in this book too. This book will disappoint you if you expect hacks, hopeful thoughts or fluffy quotes. This book is about strategies. This book will almost compel you to ponder over a few pointers. So gear up!!

Idea 1: This book is intended for a journey towards positive change, towards growth and not an attempt to judge or criticize; neither self nor others.

Idea 2: You are under no obligation to agree with all that is discussed here. Let us agree to disagree and move on....

Idea 3: This is not a book to start reading today and finish by end of the week. NO. This is a tool loaded with strategies. Read, re – read and then re – read.

Idea 4: Information is huge here. It is perfectly fine if you don't remember everything in first attempt. It has taken a decade for this book to shape up; you too need to give yourself sometime to let this seep in. Breathe and continue. Don't get mad at yourself or feel discouraged. Instead, make this an opportunity to grow, acknowledge mistakes and get better.

Idea 5: Read with a smile on your face and a highlighter in hand.

Here we go!!!! It's time to get noticed!!!

ONE ... TWO ... THREE ...

Count this in your head, One... Two... Three... this is the time most of us as humans take to form an impression about the other person. If you fail to make your mark or be visible in those precious three seconds, you are lost, Remember, "If you are lost, you are not seen"!! Acknowledge this opportunity to make yourself visible and appreciate it by taking some action to be noticed during that window of three seconds.

The moment you are seen, when you are noticed, there is an impression you leave, on the minds of people who have noticed you. And we all are aware that these impressions are long lasting. They play a pivotal role in the opportunities we gain or lose in our lives. Impressions linger on mind for much longer than you assume it will. More than that, let's understand, visual memory holds for longer duration in your brain and also that it gets recalled faster. It might seem unfair; nevertheless, it is a fact. You may like it or not, a book is often judged by its cover.

This only alarms you that even before you get a chance to greet the other person, tonnes of information and data (actually assumptions) are downloaded in the mind of other person. The potential employer has already hired you or fired you; future partner has rejected you even without knowing you well. We have endless stories revolving around this fact.

Scientists identify the Neural Circuitry of First Impressions

Scientific studies at New York University and Harvard University (2009) confirmed that people make judgements about us in just few short seconds after meeting us. Not only they judge us, in fact there are various different areas where they judge us. Entire study has been done to identify the neural circuitry of forming first impressions.

They will judge you on various areas like your economic level, the easiest and fastest to do. They even judge your education based on how you present yourself. Somewhere your competency, honesty, credibility also comes out of those snap judgements. This allows people to believe you, to trust you.

Based on that they decide your success in their mind, which may be a fact, may not be . Your sophistication is measured in the way you are seen and you present yourself. Few people are just a treat to your eyes and a few are unfortunately sore eye. People judge your political preferences, religious preferences, sexual preferences, social background and what not. The list might seem exhaustive to you, however, I am sure, I have missed on some more judgements. All this put together decides your likeability quotient.

WHAT DO YOU THINK YOUR IMAGE TELLS THE WORLD?

Does this mean that it is all about how you present, are you being noticed or not and hence, what you say does not matter? Does this mean that my other skills, education, expertise, exposure and experience are of no or less value?

Well, let us get the clarity before we get ahead. I agree, it might just look a little exaggerated, but studies do suggest that approximately 93% of how people judge us when meeting face-to-face is decided upon our non-verbal presentation. Our body language and the way we present ourselves. So then what about the words that we speak? Those only account for 7% or so. Realities hit hard, don't they?

This is based on the study by a UCLA professor, Albert Mehrabain. This study does raise a few speculations since it is understood less and misunderstood more. The study purely talks about the non-verbal signs in communication.

At no point in time will your appearance overpower the actual words, however if it is just three seconds that you have to get noticed, just three seconds to be seen, let us agree there is hardly anything other than your self-presentation and body language that does the talking.

If you can make an impact within the available three seconds, you get an opportunity to prove other abilities and competencies you have. Your verbal excellence will not really help you in the short span of three seconds.

IT IS NOT FAIR
TO BE JUDGED ON FIRST IMPRESSIONS ALONE!

Absolutely unfair!! I completely agree, but, we all do it. We invariably make judgements about all the different aspects discussed earlier. Everyone makes judgements about a person's character, credibility, intelligence, income based on what they see rather based on how you make yourself seen.

And complicating matters further; confirmation bias makes sure that the other person is likely to ignore any signs that go against the first impression they have formed in their minds. They just ignore those signs and want to stick to the first impression they formed.

However, they are extremely sensitive to signs or indicators that support their initial take on the type of person you are. If you give out cues that match their assumptions they instantly validate the image they have formed in their mind. People are little slow to pick up the cues that go against their perception of you. Hence, changing your first impression is a mammoth task.

"YOU DON'T GET A SECOND CHANCE TO MAKE A FIRST IMPRESSION."

Seriously!! First Impressions once formed are tough to change. They are almost in concrete. We tend to look for validations for the first impressions we form. We do not really go out to hunt for evidence to our initial conclusion of the first impressions formed.

The most popular thing with major Image Consultants across the globe is the holistic perspective of setting the ABCD of an individual's Image. For a professional, this also counts as a major bite of their personal brand.

The required four components to your professional image/personal brand will be:

Appearance–
How do you look?

Appearance encompasses all the things that the other individual looks into you. It is how you are seen, how are you presenting yourself.

Behaviour–
How you act?

Behaviour encompasses all the things related to your behaviour. Attitude and conduct towards others count here.

Communication–
How you talk?

Communication encompasses your ability to comprehend and converse.

Digital Footprint–
Web Presence

Digital footprint encompasses your overall presence on internet on all social media platforms you operate from.

IN CONCLUSION:
YOUR IMAGE IS
SO MUCH MORE THAN YOUR APPEARANCE

Every act and each word you say contributes towards the image you create. It plays a vital role in deciding whether you will be seen or you will be lost. Appearance, being the first access to other people it becomes vital. If you stumble on appearance aspect, it becomes difficult to be perceived as a professional in spite of articulated communication and impeccable behaviour. Against that, if your appearance works in your favour, the strong first impression lends you some lieu in terms of your communication and behavioural skills.

Hence: Appearance First!!

YOUR IMAGE IS THE STEPING STONE TO SUCCESS

DRESS TO EXPRESS

For all your important occasions, your meetings with the decision makers – both in real world or in digital world, your impression plays a vital role. This can include your boss, your team mates, your potential client or even potential partner. As discussed, your appearance is the foot in the door. People unknowingly, at a sub-conscious level pick up cues from your appearance and interpret that, without asking for any clarifications or inputs from you. If you show up in non-ironed clothes, even without asking you the reason for that, people assume you to be careless. This can be a perception, however, for the other person this is a reality. After all, perception is reality.

To add fuel to the fire, it is followed by halo effect. Here, based on one perception that people form in their minds, they assume lot of other information about you. This also will influence the amount of respect and trust you earn from other individual. Sloppy dressing leads to a perception of you being sloppy in work as well. Our image is our non-verbal communication and is highly influencing. It speaks louder than the words we speak.

The way you present yourself!

Before you shake hands there is something about your image that has already shaken the minds of the person you are dealing with. And while you are being considered for managerial positions, leadership positions, this will have a huge say. You might sound too timid and someone who will be avoiding conflicts just because you are shy. Perception might even make the other person feel that you are reluctant to take action. More than a leader, you will look like a follower. This helps people decide if you are going to stand up assertively or just give in and be spineless.

It is not only about you

It is also about the company you work for – whether you are an owner or an employee. The way you carry yourself talks a lot about what are your values; do you sacrifice important things like your dressing, makeup, shave, hair and so on to be on time. It talks about your lethargy. Having a positive and impactful impression helps you to leave everyone – bosses, co-workers, clients, vendors with the best possible perception of you and eventually your company.

APPEARENCE

Appearance at the workplace

Your looks shout before your merits can speak. One major mistake people make is thinking appearance is just clothing. NO!! It also includes other important aspects like your posture, stride, facial expressions, nail, tonality of voice, overall neatness and so on.

Sadly, people may not notice when you do these things, but they do notice when you do not do them.

Here are more than hundred tips to make that powerful first impression that helps you to be noticed in the crowd.

- **Bad Breath:** Remember that food or drinks can lead to bad breath quickly. To ensure that you do not face this problem, you make sure to either brush or at least gargle before any important meeting. Alternatively, you want to make sure to have breath – fresheners with you at all times if brushing your teeth is not possible.

- **Check your Teeth:** If you are having lunch meeting or post lunch meeting make sure you check your teeth. Food stuck in teeth is gross.

- **Filthy Shoes:** There are too many people who ignore their shoes, assuming that just wearing nice shoes with their outfit is enough. Remember that unpolished or scuffed shoes detract from your professional image.

- **Professional Pen:** Asking for a pen during an interview or meeting, looks unprepared and unprofessional. Also, do not get a pen that makes you look like a college kid. Black and blue are professionally accepted ink colours.

- **Briefcase/Bag:** Remember that these bags matter both ways; inside and outside. You do not want to open up your bag to show the mess you have. Also, get a neat, structured bag that looks professional.

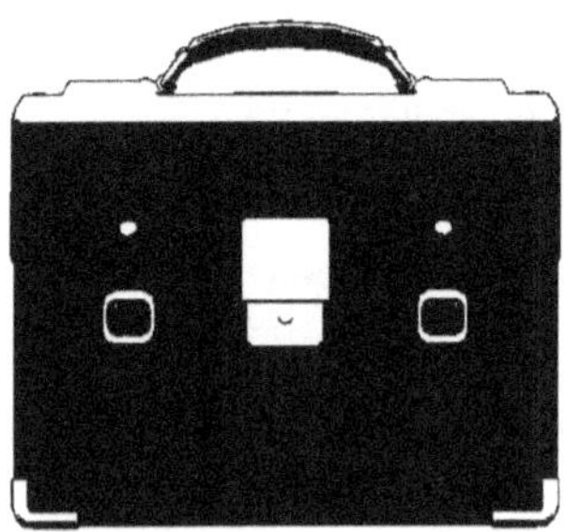

- **Coffee/Tea Stains:** This makes you look careless and unprofessional. Use a paper tissue underneath cup to save from such stains.

- **Hair:** Remember that hair frames your face. With right kind of a hairdo to suit your facial features, you will look sharp.

- **The Finer Details:** People are going to notice the smaller details such as shirt is not ironed, or tie knot is not crisp. Take care of the details since devil lies in details.

- **Tattoos/Piercing:** While you may claim that it is a part of who you are, it is your personality it definitely does not give you a professional image. Cover the tattoos, if you have any and leave behind the piercings while at work.

- **Watch:** Ensure you have a conservative watch and nothing too big, too colourful, too bling.

Appearance alone will never determine success but it plays a major role in your success. Not only does your appearance help you get a job, it can also help you be owned by your company for a much longer time. Here, it is not about being good-looking but the focus is on looking good – looking presentable. It is integral to look part for whatever your role is at the workplace. People might just give up on you, might lose their trust in you, because it feels like you don't take care for your appearance. We have all heard, "don't judge the book by its cover" True, we should not pre-judge anyone by the way they look, however; for most of us, at most of the times, this is how our life and our business work. Largely, based on snap judgements.

- **Facial Hair:** It is never a problem till you keep it well groomed. Beard and moustache need extra care.

- **Hair:** Hair should be neat and groomed – all the times. Visit your hair dresser regularly depending upon the growth and style of the hair you maintain.

- **Tags and Stitching:** You might be just surprised to learn how many people just leave their tags on suits. The back stich in blazers needs to go before you wear them.

- **Cologne:** Remember that you want to just have a pleasant smell, not that your smell lingers for four hours even after you leave. Go easy on this.

- **Nails:** Men may choose not go for manicures but they definitely need neat and trimmed nails. Nail biting is another no-no.

- **Jewelry:** Jewelry for men in a professional arena is still a grey area. Keep it minimal and professional. Avoid any piece that becomes a distraction.

- **Wallet:** Make sure you preferably have a leather wallet in black/brown colour. Do not stuff things in your wallet. When shoved in the back pocket, this disturbs the contours of body.

- **Belt:** Use this as a stand out piece. Replace belt once it start to run down. It is a good idea to have one black and one brown belt in order to complete your basic professional wardrobe.

- **Suit and Shirt**: Suits are extremely professional. One can hardly go wrong while wearing a dark suit with light coloured shirt.

- **Shirt Sleeves:** As tricky as it can be. Full sleeves for suits are professional. While wearing full sleeves, it is advisable not to fold the sleeves. Half sleeves are accepted, however not for very formal occasions and never with suits.

- **Tie:** With tie, invest in classics. Do not fall into the trap of trends. Ties in silk are most professional.

- **Wrinkles:** Wearing wrinkled clothes shout out that you don't care. Look for the wrinkle free fabrics. If you can, do consider avoiding pure cotton and linen for your work wear.

- **Dry Clean:** It is popularly believed, dry clean is the best garment care. However, it is a myth. Read care label to figure out what is the best care for that particular fabric.

The way you dress becomes all the more important because it not only affects how other people perceive you, but also influences how you think of yourself. The moment you look the part, you start behaving the part. This increases your confidence. In return your peers, your seniors; your team starts to respect you as a reaction to your strong impression.

Being noticed has its own perks. The undeniable truth is being good – looking is helpful. Always and for everyone.

- **Eyebrows:** They are an important facial feature and helps express yourself. Take care of the shape and maintain them properly.

- **Make Up:** At work it is not supposed to look made up. For work purpose keep it minimal. Anything that is too colourful, too bright, too heavy, too glittery is for occasions other than work.

- **Perfume:** Some people are sensitive to odour, be conservative in the amount of perfume you use and the smell you choose. Do not go overboard.

- **Jewelry:** Feel free to use some jewellery, however keep it minimal. Avoid things that can tangle, make noise or dangle a lot. It becomes distraction for others.

- **Purse:** While looking for a purse to carry at workplace, look for neutral colours and structured shapes. Select the interior of the purse to suit your specific needs.

- **Skirts:** When you choose a skirt-suit or simply a skirt, be mindful of hemline. While standing the bare minimum is your skirt reaches the knee.

- **Underneath your jacket:** It is underneath but it is visible. For workplace a shirt, blouse or a traditional shell is a better choice.

- **Shoes:** Choose a pair of shoe that is closed against open sandals. Absolutely flat and stilettos; both are not for workplace. Keep your shoes neat clean and in shape. Flip flops cannot be worn at work.

- **Pantyhose:** Make sure that your pantyhose does not have a run in it. Not a bad idea to carry one extra, in case you might just need that.

- **Accessories:** Add up some classic and quality pieces to your work wear. Accessories are like vitamins, they help. As a caution, do not over accessories.

- **High Heels:** High heels are great mood changer. They change your posture, stride and attitude. However learn to walk in them; you don't want to appear like a new born calf learning to walk.

- **Chipped Nail/Nail paint:** Take care your nails are clean, well painted or not painted. Neutral colours in nail paints are more appreciated at workplace.

Several Studies show that more attractive people are, on average, wealthier and have higher-paying jobs than less attractive people. Sadly, true. Many of these studies are summarized and discussed in the 2011 book "Beauty Pays: Why Attractive People Are More Successful" written by Daniel Hamermesh, an economist at the University of Texas in Austin.

The research reviewed by Hamermesh shows that attractive people earn an average of 3 or 4% more than people with below average looks. Beautiful people get hired sooner, get promotions more quickly, are higher-ranking in their companies, and get all kinds of extra benefits. Turns out that more attractive people often bring more money to their companies and therefore are more valuable employees.

- **Hair:** Hair should be worn neat. Depending on your hair length, work environment and the way you wear your hair, you may choose to let your hair loose. Any sparkly hair accessories, glitter, messy hair is seen as unprofessional.

- **Teeth Whitening:** With smoking, frequent tea/coffee intake teeth might just start to yellow. Investing in some whitening treatment and taking care of teeth adds to your presence.

- **Dandruff**: This is not painful so we think it is harmless. However, it is a dent to your first impression. Work wear normally being in dark colours, the dandruff is distinctly visible.

- **Toss or Tailor your Pants:** Check all of them closely. Are there any with open hems, are they too long or too tight, if yes - they need to either go to tailor or toss them.

- **Trim them:** Check your nose, ear, neck and if you see any hair in the mirror, others see it too. Get a clipper and get rid of those extras.

- **Dyed Hair:** You may choose to dye your hair, but take care of the colours you choose. Unnatural colours do look unprofessional, if you work in a traditional work area. Browns are best suited for professional look. If you can, get your hair professionally dyed against doing it yourself.

- **Check your Back:** We never fail to have a glance in mirror before leaving. That is the last minute check, sadly only for the front side. Get into habit of checking your backside as well.

- **Do not overuse hair products:** The worst thing to do is not using any products and the second worst is over use of the same. The crunchy hair look is just not professional. Spare that.

- **Thinning Hair:** Our lifestyles with high stress and no discipline can gift us thinning hair a little earlier than expected. Get some hair cut to compliment the thinning and start taking care before it is too late.

- **Stop Branding Others:** Do not get carried away and advertise the logos of other brands just because you invested huge money in buying that.

- **Ditch the Backpack:** Comfortable as it may be, certainly not professional. Save that for your next holiday but don't carry it to work. Invest in a good structured bag for work.

- **Hide your Underwear:** Nobody is interested in brand you wear or colours you choose. Just hide them. Seriously, hide them.

- **DRESS UP:** Always dress up and never dress down. Look at people who are at the positions you want to reach. Dress like them or maybe better!

Power Moves for Appearance

- In a professional scenario use lighter color in the top garment and darker color in bottom garment. This helps you to grab and hold attention of the person on or near your face
- It is a good idea to match the color and texture of the shoes, belt and bag you carry. It helps to have a "put together" look
- Make sure your hardware is all gold or all silver. In case you want to mix both in your look, have one piece with both the metals in order to unite the entire look.

BEHAVIOR

IMPORTANCE OF BEHAVIOUR IN THE WORKPLACE

Two important aspects to your respectable image at work place are behaviour and ethics. Your appearance helps you to build a strong image but that image is sustained only with the expected behaviour according to the industry norms. Behaviour will generally include attire, interaction, language used, ability to handle situations, etc. each of these traits are equally important.

- **A Weak Handshake:** It is a complete no – no. It does not matter, in work arena, if you meet a man or a woman, just make a good eye contact, flash a smile and give a firm hand shake. Firm doesn't mean bone crushing, by the way!

- **Invading Personal Space:** Be aware of the concept of personal space. Don't be right in the face of people when you are supposed to keep distance. This can be extremely uncomfortable for many.

- **Crossing your Arms:** Conservatively, this is taken as sounding defensive, closed or even uncomfortable when you are meeting someone for the first time. Even if you are not an old school, it is always good to have open hands and palms.

- **Lack of Eye Contact**: Maintain a healthy eye contact while you are being introduced, when other person is speaking so that you pay attention. Treat eye contact as a connection tool with the other person.

- **Not Smiling Enough:** It is not expected to burst in laughter and crack jokes, however, not having any smile at all at your work place – whether it is an interview, meeting or a coffee break – tags you as either nervous or unfriendly.

- **Smiling All the Time:** Contradictory to earlier point, few people are just smiling all the day, whatever the situation. Be mindful of when and to whom do you smile.

- **Do not Hide your Hands:** Using your hands make you more expressive and also more trustworthy. Many people tend to hide their hands, or even sit on them. Never do that.

THERE IS A LOT
WE CAN DO TO MAKE A GOOD FIRST IMPRESSION

Dressing nicely and communicating properly with the people we meet are just two options. Few other aspects also play an important role in how someone is going to remember you. Some of these suggestions may not be applicable to all in context of creating a powerful first impression, however; they can be highly helpful while going for an interview or for important meetings.

- **Read the Mood**: Observe the people closely. Try to figure out broadly what that person can likely be. If they are a little casual, you may be casual as well. If they appear formal, you too need to be more formal.

- **Having Your Seat**: It is a good idea to look for an acknowledgment if not permission before you sit. This is plain good manners and shows consideration.

- **Do not Exaggerate:** Make sure to maintain a balance. Moderation is the key in behaviour. Keep a look at your gestures, if they are going all out. Practise mirroring since it shows nonverbal agreement.

- **Be prepared:** Before you meet someone, go for interview, make sure you do enough research about them. That will not only form a positive impression on them but will also instantly like you.

- **Be on Time**: If you are not few minutes before time, you are late. Don't be earlier than five minutes which might cause inconvenience. Being late is a strong factor which would be considered as you being too casual and careless.

- **Plan for Possible Delays**: If you want to be on time, do not miss on this factor. Do your own reiki for your travel time depending on your mode of transport and the traffic situations at your hour of travel. In case you are way too early, go grab a cup of coffee, but do not disturb your host.

- **Turn off Cell Phones:** We love them dearly, but while meeting clients, co-workers, vendors you want to make sure it is on silent mode. Keeping phone on vibrate mode is a form of silent disturbance. Avoid it.

A POSITIVE ATTITUDE CAN CARRY YOU A LONG WAY

Possessing the necessary skills is essential but positive attitude is like cherry on cake. There are guidelines for behavior in the workplace, do you know why – because they matter. If the conduct does not follow suit it is a dent to you, your co-workers and your company. Companies pay for poor conduct in form of time, money and resources. Companies hence understand that for their people to be productive and successful, behavior, attitude and communication is one integral part.

- **Do not Drink, Eat, Smoke or Chew**: While it is perfectly fine at lunch meeting, at other occasions be mindful of doing any of this. You do not want to miss on any opportunity to speak just because your mouth is full.

- **Reach Home in Time**: Are you the one to leave office last and also feel proud of it? Think again. This is not being dedicated; this means you are not competent to finish your task in designated time. Be focused on work while at office and leave on time. Exceptions are always there, but they are once in a while.

- **Shake Hands First:** It is imperative to shake hands in business situations, irrespective of the gender. The interesting thing here is to note that one who initiates the handshake wins the Power game.

- **Learn to Bend:** You may not bend in terms of your values, but bend a bit while you are being introduced. It just shows your humility. Do not bend enough that people would walk over.

NEGATIVE BEHAVIOR TRANSLATES FASTER

When dealing with a team, negative behavior is a fast to catch trait. Our office interaction is one of the biggest aspects affected by behavior. A positive and respectable behavior earns you better relationships; more respect and hence team is happy and productive when with you, and opposite is equally true. Negative behavior will be picked up fast and replicated faster. People with poor behavior are hence not considered for senior positions. Take care of that.

- **Play the Game:** Think of your business or work as your favorite sport. Follow the rules of the game and still have the fun, whether it is business or sport. That is an analogy to think over.

- **Stand Up Straight:** Parents and school teachers taught us about this and they were bang on. It makes you look confident, in charge, full of self – pride and also keeps your spine in a good condition.

- **Introduce Others**: It is pleasure to be introduced by others, which means people know you. Feel blessed but at the same time, do not forget the ones who need to be introduced. Go ahead and introduce them to others, they will love you for this gesture.

- **Spend Some Money:** Is it your employee's birthday? Or maybe someone is in hospital. Something as simple as a lunch or basket of fruit goes long way in spite of not digging your pockets deep. Be comfortable with spending for them. They are your support system.

- **Widen Your Stance :** If you stand with your feet just next to each other, you can seem unsure of yourself. Apart from this it is uncomfortable. Widen your stance, relax your knees and distribute your weight equally to look in control.

- **Try a Steeple:** We see many politicians, actors, trainers, coaches, posing in steeple. Give it a try when you want to sound absolutely confident about what are you saying.

- **Sit up Straight**: Lean forward a bit and sit straight. This shows you are engaged and interested in the conversation. Sit facing towards the person so that you both can see each other completely.

Power Moves for Behavior

- Love and Respect for other people is the triumph card. It is the ultimate power. Practice it
- There is no map to behavior, be prepared to adapt according to the situation and people involved
- Your behavior is a reflection of your own values, education, judgments, beliefs etc. It is about you and not the other person involved. Be mindful of it

COMMUNICATION

THE IMPORTANCE OF COMMUNICATION
IN THE WORKPLACE

After the first three seconds, the person now has an opinion about you. This also means that even before you speak the other person already has made up his/her mind about you, positive or negative.

When it comes to communication, we feel it is all about the spoken words. However, it is more about the tonality of voice. It is not only about "what you say", it is much more about "how you say it".

When used correctly, communication can be your key to greater success. It helps you develop positive business relationships, influence and motivate your team. It helps improve productivity, bond with team members and present ideas with better impact.

Knowing this, we will dwell into the communication aspect of making a good first impression on someone you have never met before.

- **Relax your Voice:** Quality of your voice can be a deciding factor. High pitch might be just taken as nervous, less empathic and less powerful.

- **Speak Clearly:** Studies say we are better impressed with people who speak clearly. This makes it easy for the brain to seep the information when communication is clear.

- **Be comfortable with Silence:** Do not attempt to fill those moments of silence with useless chit chat. Remember silence is clear. Unnecessary blabbering leads to revealing more than necessary information and that is unprofessional.

- **Focus on What to Say:** Voice modulation is the key. Monotone makes you appear boring. Speak at moderate pace and annunciate clearly.

- **Speak the Language:** Unless you are into a technical conversation, do not use jargons and slang. This displays your knowledge and technical expertise. Not everybody understands that.

- **Avoid Fillers:** The whole series of unnecessary words such as "like" or "you know" or the uh and hmm are fillers. It indicates you are either hunting for words or not sure of what to speak. They make you look and sound unpolished.

- **A Happy Friendly Face:** Keep your expressions in alignment with spoken words. In case of contradiction, people will only trust the expressions and doubt your words, however true they are.

- **Check facial Expressions:** Some expressions that are easy to identify are : sad, happy, surprise, fear, disgust, anger and contempt. It is not easy to conceal expressions but be aware of the listed expressions since they easily show up on the face and people identify them in seconds.

- **Expressionless Face:** When you are nervous or tense is when you have an expressionless face. Practise some simple expression like smile and how to shake off the nervousness.

EFFECTIVE COMMUNICATION IS A BUSINESS TOOL

Communication is sharing information and ideas between individuals or groups so as to reach a common understanding. With information overload, varied personalities, different mind-sets and ideas, effective communication is certainly a challenge for business owners, CEO's, Managers and Employees. Companies identify communication as an attribute which is needed to meet its objectives. When all members of a team, department communicate effectively; productivity increases, a better workplace environment is created. And objectives are met more effectively.

- **Use Person's Name:** What is more loving than a person's name for him/her? Make it a point to address people by their name during a conversation. If the name sounds foreign to you, ask them how are you supposed to pronounce it.

- **Having More than One Person to Talk to:** In business scenario it is common to talk to more than one person at the same time. Meetings, conferences, network events, interview, all of these places you might have to do so. Gaze at all of them, one after the other. In case of a question, start with the person asking question, gaze at all and return to the same person to finish your answer.

- **Do Not Rub or Touch your Nose:** Traditionally this is considered as a strong sign of person speaking lie.

- **Do not rub your Neck or Head**: These behaviors are associated with disinterest or indecisiveness. Resist the itch or cramp if you can.

- **Do Not Shake your Legs:** This not only works as a distraction it also signals that you are not comfortable, you are probably nervous.

- **Do not Slouch in Your Seat**: This shows you are disinterested. You want to quit the conversation and move out. It indicates that you sound unprepared and not bothered.

- **Do not Stand in Scissor Stance**: This only means you want to linger. You are not ready or you are not willing to take a decision. This takes your power away.

- **Show Interest**: Do not appear as a bubblehead. Make sure to keep an interested expression. Nod occasionally and give out some positive expressions.

PROJECTING A POWERFUL IMAGE DOES NOT JUST HAPPEN; IT HAS TO BE CULTIVATED

- **Avoid Seeming Judgemental:** You do not have to necessarily agree or disagree every time with the values, ideas or opinions of people. However, you do need to stop being judgemental about it. Criticism will block your ability to understand the other person's point of view.

- **Observe Them:** Learn by observing people at public places like metro stations, malls, restaurant etc. you can watch some television programs while you mute the voice and try to decode the body language. These exercises will give you practical inputs of what to do and what not to. Learn from others mistakes instead of making them yourself.

- **Deliver Bad News in Person:** Written communication does not give you an option to soften your difficult messages with the right use of non-verbal. Bad news delivered in person helps since there is lot of comfort and empathy along with the bad news.

- **I am Not Joking:** Please consider not to share inappropriate jokes or any form of humour that makes people uncomfortable.

- **Do Not Cry:** Figure a better way to express your emotions. Tears put you in a weak spot. It is ok to be vulnerable but tears are not welcome. You would generally not be considered for leadership positions.

- **Do Not Swear:** This is no brainer. You are looked down in a professional scenario if you have the habit of swearing.

- **Do Not Flirt:** Flirting cannot be the currency in office. This can be easily taken in wrong way by the concerned person and the co-workers. Once you indulge in such activities, people treat this as an open invitation. Beware!!

- **Giggling:** We all know the difference between giggle and smile!! Appropriate laughter is a major indicator of Gravitas.

- **Think Global:** Certain phrases and slang are country specific. An Asian understands and talks different than a American and a European. Avoid local country or region slangs and talk neutral and international language.

- **Listen carefully:** Let us understand communication is a two-way process and at times listening can be more important than speaking.

EFFECTIVE COMMUNICATION
IS A SKILL THAT CAN BE LEARNED

Follow all of the discussed tips and you will be better at communication, since it is a learnable skill. The way you communicate sets a precedent for the company, hence your communication needs to be clear, persuasive and concise. Learn to communicate effectively and you will be able to set yourself apart and opportunities will come your way more frequently.

Power Moves for Communication

- Spoken grace is a great tool, experiment using it as often as you can
- Ability to ask the right question at right time is one skill to be acquired
- Never confuse communication with language. Language is just a medium to communicate

DIGITAL PRESENCE

THE IMPORTANCE OF DIGITAL FOOTPRINT
IN THE WORKPLACE

These days our online image has become all the more important than ever. Before we meet anyone in person, the person has already been through our online presence, social media platforms, Google search, and Company website and so on. Offline or in-person impression gets influenced by the online image that is created before meeting the person.

In Google age privacy is not even a luxury, you might think your professional and personal lives are different, but they are merged on social media.

People can access your posts, pictures; about me sections on any social media platform and make an impression about you based on any post. It can be political post, religious post, family post, offhand topics and so on. Online impressions are equally powerful and permanent hence need attention.

- **Google Search Your Name:** This is your first step to get started to check your digital image. This will help you understand where you stand and what people see in your name.

- **Be mindful of your Social Circles**: Friday parties are to be enjoyed, not to be necessarily posted on Social Media. Check if you are tagged in any inappropriate photos.

- **Did You get that Job**: Did you bag that big client? Brilliant, but does it necessarily go on social media? Check and double check before putting things online. It can be against the policy of a company or a client.

- **Create a Google Alert in Your Name:** Anytime there is information added about you, you will be informed right away. Use the technology.

- **Images too Count:** Do a Google Image Search in your name and either you will be glad or glared. Either ways it will help you.

- **Do not Overshare:** Sharing is caring but do not forget anything in excess is poison. Think if anyone else except you would be excited about your post.

- **Too Little Posts:** Do not neglect the power of social media. Out of sight is out of mind. Keep posting since you don't want to be lost.

- **Always Online:** It looks like you hardly have anything else to do. Restrict your social media hours for this one reason also, apart from being more productive and focused.

- **Keep it Balanced:** Keep your content balanced. Post on various topics with enough variety. Idea is to create interest, not call for controversy and so be mindful of your content.

- **Stay Positive:** Do not use social media as a place to hash out your frustrations. Everyone is frustrated, not just you. Use the space in a responsible way.

When used accurately, your social media can help you curate an online professional image. Social media gives a peep into your personality to people even before they meet you. They are now partly prepared what to expect upon meeting you. Keep your digital footprint crisp and clear and you will reap rewards.

- **Do Not be Inappropriate:** What looks funny to you might be a disgust to others, might be humiliation to someone else. Be extra cautious to check the appropriateness for a public platform.

- **Everything is Public:** Private word is out of vocabulary when it comes to social media. Once posted it is cyber property and practically can never be deleted.

- **Update your Profile:** Do this regularly. Keep all information current and updated.

- **Privacy Settings:** Keep a check on your privacy settings often and adjust them appropriately. If you have something that others should not see, make sure they do not. Best is to not have that content online, second best is to safeguard well.

- **Wrong Timed Posting:** The time you post also reveals a lot. While at work you better work and not post on social media. Family crisis is another time to show respect and not post just anything.

- **Keep a Current Picture:** Surely, we all looked way better when we were younger, but posting those photos as display or profile picture might be taken as a deception by people. Keep a current picture so people can relate with you in person.

- **Cover Photos:** Remember, this is what people see first. Put an appropriate picture of yours and not your pet or a sunset picture or a quote.

- **Being too Pushy:** Refrain from sharing strong opinions about sensitive topics. You may have your own ideas, stick to them but do not post them. As a thumb rule, avoid topics like politics, religion and sex.

- **Tag Only if Allowed:** Remember to take consent if you need to tag people. Unless they are a part of the picture or are related to the story, avoid tagging. If you tag, seek permission before doing that.

- **Get Permission to Post:** Lots of work related information needs a prior permission for posting online. Make sure you do not land in a soup only out of the urge to post something in haste.

- **Review your Post:** Check twice for spell check, grammatical error before you post it. Make sure the message conveyed is what you want to convey and not misplaced.

- **A Complete Profile:** Be sure to fill out all the details in your profile. This makes the profile powerful. It tells people that you have invested time in filling profile and it matters to you.

- **Multiple Profiles:** Avoid confusing people with multiple profiles, unless that is exactly what you want to do. Having one profile will also help you to focus and work on it hence making it sharp and professional.

- **Give Credit:** It is perfectly fine to share stuff on social media from other's pages and profiles or websites, but do not forget to give due credits. This makes you look ethical, trustworthy and responsible individual.

- **ALL CAPS:** THIS WILL MAKE PEOPLE THINK YOU ARE MAD AT THEM AND YELLING AT THEM, THE WAY YOU ARE FEELING RIGHT NOW. Avoid it. It is not easy on eyes to read all capital. Use sentence case.

- **Spammy:** Do not keep sharing same stuff too often. This is spam. This will annoy your followers. They will stop following you or might just lose their like and respect for you.

- **No Automated Messages**: They sound robotic and stiff. Keep social media, social. Make your messages original and they will stand out for the right reasons.

- **You do not have to Friend Everyone:** Some people think more the merrier, whereas quality of your connections and friends is more important. Who you connect with talks about who you are, hence be careful of your connections.

- **Do not Ignore the Little Things**: What you share, what you like and what comments you put is what people are watching. Think twice before you act.

- **Keep it Clean:** Do not get into filthy discussions or use of abusive language. People forget the context but remember what levels you drop to.

Power Move for Digital Presence

- Digitally, keep personal and professional separate when it comes to being professional in using digital medium
- Own your social media presence; let it not be by default. Design it with effort and time
- Look for a happy medium. Neither too less – Nor too much is the key to impactful digital presence.

LET US ALSO DWELL INTO THE CONSEQUENCES OF AN UNPROFESSIONAL IMAGE

- **Disrespect from Others:** You might fall victim to mockery around the workplace regarding your attire, behaviour or communication. You might even pay high price in terms of being disregarded for higher positions. You might want to fight this saying, It is not right, It is unfair, It is unethical, but the only fact is that it happens!!

- **Distraction from your Work:** If your attire, your behaviour and/or your communication is distracting to others, they get annoyed and concerned about those aspects more than concentrating on you and your work. You just end up distracting people from your work. Your image is now working against you.

- **Loss in Business:** While you are meeting your clients and you are unfortunately not appropriately dressed and/or behaved, you might just end up losing on that opportunity of sales. Client in that situation fails to trust you, your capabilities and credibility.

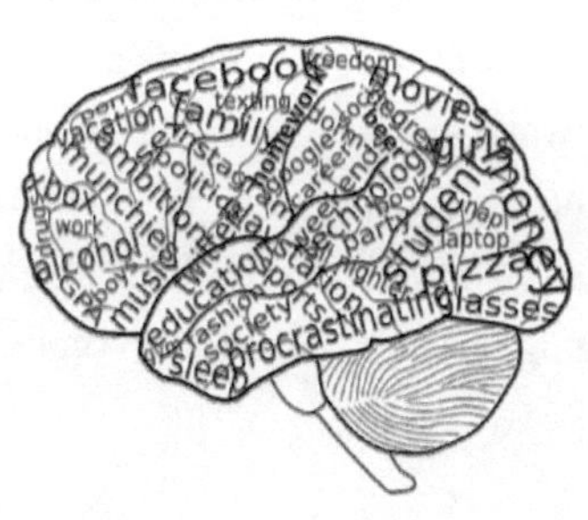

- **Sexual Harassment:** A sensitive issue at workplace, for employees and employer. One might feel great about his/her body but workplace is not a place to display that pride in the way you dress for work. Lot of people do that unknowingly as well. Be aware of the communication your image is doing in order to appear a person in charge and feel safe.

- **Feeling Leftout:** Companies these days operate more like a gigantic sport team. You need to fit into this team in your own capacity. If your image is not up to the mark, people might just be averse to you thinking you are not a part of them. The feeling of being leftout eventually impacts your productivity and personality as well.

- **Missing opportunities:** One of the major consequences of not taking care of your image at work is endless list of missed opportunities. Not getting a job in spite of high grades, not being promoted in spite of performance, being rejected for major proposals, not being appreciated for your work and your credentials and list goes on and on. One of the reasons could be something related to you being seen or are you always lost. Are you being noticed or being ignored is something that depends on your image.

SO, DO YOU NEED AN IMAGE CONSULTANT?

You probably have heard the adage "dress for the job you want, not the job you have." One of the best ways to improve the overall appearance that you present on a daily basis is by hiring an image consultant to overhaul your entire image. When people hear the term "image consultant", it often conjures up images of a specialist who comes to your home or place of business and makes sure that you look your best, that your wardrobe matches the image that you are trying to present to others.

But, it's not just selecting a wardrobe. It is much more. It is about mentoring, guiding, coaching, and educating people through the science and art of image management. While an image consultant certainly addresses fashion as well, it goes far beyond that. It is about communicating in a way that presents your message in an articulate and professional manner; it is about maintaining a professional image at all times. An image consultant empowers clients to project the confidence and competence needed in order to make an appropriate and authentic appearance for any professional, social, or private situation.

CAN YOU AFFORD IT?

The first thing that people wonder about when they hear the term image consultant is, "can I afford to hire someone to work on my image?" Even though it is not polite to answer a question with a question, it suits this particular case: can you afford not to?

Increased competition in the job market has become commonplace. You do not have the luxury to mess up with those initial 3 seconds of meeting someone. That is when you want to ensure, you are seen.

DO I LOSE MY SENSE OF SELF?

Some people feel that they may lose their personal sense of self if they hire an image consultant. However, you have to keep in mind that anything an image consultant presents to you is advice, not a direct order. A professional image consultant will sit down with you, talk about what motivates you, what your aspirations are, what your experiences are. Then they will provide advice based on that. They are not going to change you into something you are not; they are going to help you improve on what you are already doing. They are going to emphasize the positives instead of trying to change you into something that you are not.

EVERYONE CAN BENEFIT

It does not matter if you are fresh out of college, recently unemployed, or have worked with the same company for a decade, or own a company, anyone can benefit from working with an image consultant. Keep in mind that for many people an image consultant is not necessarily an expense but an investment that can help you stand out from all the other people currently in the market.

Ultimately, you decide whether you believe that an image consultant can help you. Would you want that after years from now you will sit back and think about how those few short hours could have made a difference, could have helped you stand out and achieve the career that you were hoping for? It is your career, it is your image, and you decide whether you want to make the most out of it or not.

MEGHAVI VYAS

Meghavi Vyas holds an international certification in Image Management, Styling and Wardrobe Management from Conselle – Utah, USA. After her Civil Engineering she continued to work with added knowledge of Vastu Shastra. It did not take her long to realize that she can design and align energies for others; but she herself needed a redesign or realignment for her life. That is when she stumbled upon the – at that time new - concept of image management. She just took a leap of faith and got into this whole heartedly.

Back in 2010 was when she took this plunge and eventually graduated as an Image Management Consultant from Image Consulting Business Institute.

To add to her credentials, she also added a prestigious Soft Skill Certification accredited by Scotland government body – S.Q.A. and her Train the Trainer is accredited by S.Q.A. as well as Indian Quality Council body – NABET.

Today, after a decade, she has moved from engineering buildings to engineering personalities. Meghavi firmly believes in her brand promise that quotes, "Change your Image, Change your Life". Her mission in life is to help people get noticed. She often quotes, she is into the work of people packaging. She has been a proud recipient of Asean Business Excellence Award by IeCM Malaysia in year 2017 as an advancing entrepreneur from India. Twice in a row, 2019 – 2020 she has been recognised and awarded as one amongst the top 150 woman entrepreneurs pan India by Great Companies. She has been awarded Best Woman Entrepreneur by Live24, a national news channel in Feb 2020.

MORE ABOUT

OUR IMAGE MANAGEMENT CONSULTING SERVICES

Individual Services

- Executive Presence for Senior Management
- Image Makeover
- Corporate Styling

Group Coaching

- Power of Personal Appearance
- Power Dressing
- Etiquette to Elevate
- Speak with Joy
- Personal Brand

Corporate Services

- Uniform Design
- Tailor made sessions (Soft Skills and Image Management)

www.ingramcontent.com/pod-product-compliance
Lightning Source LLC
Chambersburg PA
CBHW020740160726
47993CB00006B/2540